WARSHIPS

WARSHIPS

showed that the USSR strategy of attacking NATO fleets with anti-ship missiles, especially aircraft carriers could be successful, while the strategy designed by NATO against the USSR during the Cold War evolved from a general naval blockade to a nuclear attack using on-board planes, long-range terrestrial airplanes and strategic nuclear missiles on board submarines or located in silos and/or terrestrial shuttles.

The USSR, on the other hand, planned to subject NATO countries to total submarine war, simultaneous to the attack of its fleets by anti-ship-missiles.

The first truly operative missiles installed on board ships were anti-aircraft SAM, Surface-Air Missiles, but with the perceived Soviet threat, all ships incorporated some form of anti-missile armament.

The gyratory launchers of the first antiaircraft missiles gave way to vertical launch silos (VLS) with greater versatility and fire-power.

CRUISERS
OR HEAVY ESCORTS

The cruiser was born at the end of the XIX century. But the denomination is confusing, especially since the beginning of the missile age.

The first cruisers

At first, the cruiser was a rapid warship, less heavily armed and protected than the battleship and with a great range for surveillance missions and to combat enemy incursions.

The cruiser's specifications allowed it to attack enemy merchant traffic and defend home traffic, and it was often used for policing colonial waters.

In 1922, the Washington Conference defined heavy cruisers as those armed with 203 mm guns, and light cruisers, those with 152 mm. An exception was the battle-cruiser whose artillery was similar to the battleship but with less armor and greater speed.

In the two World Wars, cruisers were built for specific antiaircraft tasks. These, and the destroyers with improved specifications resulting from wartime experience, which converted

them into light cruisers, and the introduction of missiles during the 1950s and 1960s, together with the ability to deploy aircraft from flight decks, confused the denomination of cruiser.

New ship, new names

In the 1950s, the US Navy designed a new type of ASW ship. The Norfolk DL-1 hull was similar to the Juneau class antiaircraft cruisers, incorporating features learned from the nuclear tests at Bikini. Designated Destroyer Leader (DL) in 1952, it was redesignated as a frigate in 1955.

Between 1952 and 1955, DL ships of the Mitscher class, entered service. Later ships, although similar were designated as DLG, due to the addition of missiles. At the same time, the US Navy built twenty-two DDG Charles. F. Adams missile destroyers.

All these ships had a high capacity/ displacement – between 4,500 and 8,800 tons fully loaded, with light artillery, anti-submarine weapons and various types of missiles.

FROM THE TICONDEROGA
TO THE DD(X)

▶ *The 'Ticonderoga' class cruisers are ships that have already been in service many years. They were the first warships to mount the new AEGIS system and they are still highly capable vessels.*

In its origins, the cruiser was a heavily armed ship, which escorted combat fleets or convoys or engaged enemy ships of equal or greater range.

Today, the future of the cruiser in the US Navy is not promising, with its main current task being to protect the aircraft carrier fleets with its electronic shield.

The Ticonderoga

To protect the aircraft carriers (baffle group) and four battleships (action group) of the US Navy at the beginning of the 1980s, at least 27 cruisers were needed, in order to reach the established norm of 1.5 heavy escorts per group.

The Ticonderoga were conceived as nuclear-powered, but Congress did not approve the

budget, and finally, the ships were powered by existing, conventional gas tubines used by the Spruance class destroyers, whose power made them ideal.

However, the ships underwent various modifications and adaptations to the interior which limited the armoring of vital areas with Kevlar.

Originally the ships were designated as missile destroyers (DDG) but were later redesignated as missile cruisers (CG) before entering service on January 22 1983.

Combat service

During the Dessert Storm and Dessert Shield operations against Iraq, the Princeton was severely damaged by two magnetic mines – probably Italian made – which exploded at the rear starboard near the stem and near one of the fins. The ship's hull was left twisted, there was severe electrical damage and the starboard engine was put out of service.

During the Iraq War in 1991, the Ticonderoga launched 105 SSM Tomahawk (Bunker Hill, 28 missiles; Normandy, 26; Mobile Bay, 22; San Jacinto, 14; Philippine Sea, 10; Princeton, 3 and

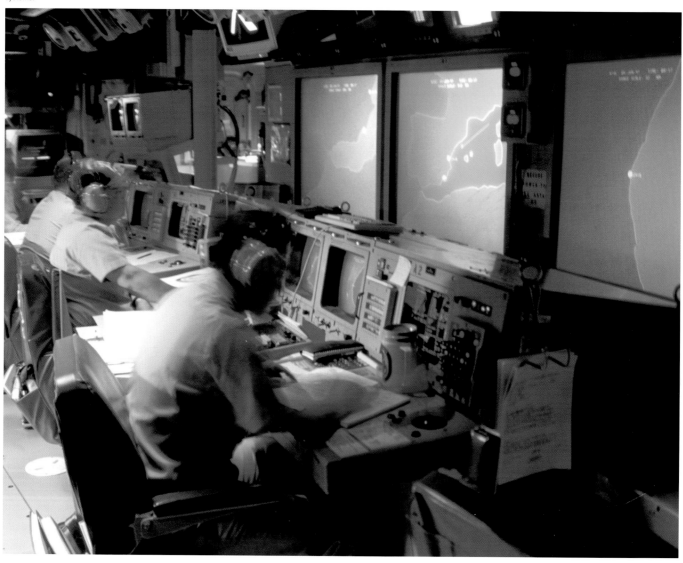

Leyte Gulf, 2). In June 1993, the Chancellorsville launched another 9 SSM Tomahawk against Iraq in a punishment operation.

In July 1988, the Vincennes became involved in a serious international incident, when it shot down a commercial Iranian jumbo jet with Standard missiles. At the time, the combat systems were on automatic control and it seems that the ship's sensors confused the jumbo with an Iranian F-14 Tomcat beginning an attack.

The Arsenal project

Since the invasion of Kuwait by Iraq in 1990, the US Navy has pursued the idea of a heavy surface ship capable of launching enough ground attack missiles to dissuade any possible aggressor. The high cost of the project has limited its development, with the category and performance being reduced from cruiser to destroyer, and with various changes of designation.

Crew numbers will be surprisingly small – perhaps as few as fifty – and the ship could be commanded from another ship or base or even a military satellite.

Recent information suggests that the project is now being merged with another known as the DD-21, 21st Century Combatant Ship or DD(X).

▼ *In the future, the U.S. Navy will include designs like the DD-X, a ship that breaks with classical warship design and introduces new technologies and capabilities.*

The DD-21/21stCCS/DD(X)

This project was born at almost the same time as the Arsenal plan, but few of its main specifications were made public, except that it should integrate efficacy and low cost and small crew numbers with discretion, modular assembly, and a multi-role capability.

Recently, the project was given land attack destroyer duties similar to the Arsenal project, and it seems the two plans have been merged into the DD(X). It is perhaps significant that, at the Euronaval Fair in October 2002, no other project was mentioned.

This new type of ship will be the substitute of the Ticonderoga, CG-47 cruisers and the Oliver H. Perry, FFG-7 frigates as well as the Spruance DD-963 and Kidd DDG-993 destroyers.

The funds for the project come from Public Law 103-160, section 845, previously used by the Defense Advanced Research Projects Agency (DARPA) for the Arsenal cruiser. The acquisition program has five phases. Phase I, the design concept phase, cost six million dollars and terminated on April 1 1998, when contracts were adjudicated. In Phase II, the initial system design phase, contracts were awarded to two companies – Bath Iron Works/Lockheed Martin GES and Ingalls Shipbuilding/Raytheon Systems Company at a cost of 45 million dollars. Phase III, system completion and subsystem design, did not reduce the contractors to one as previously

◀ The stern gun is mounted on the aft superstructure. The Ticonderoga are equipped with two four-barrel SSM Harpoon missile batteries. Also on the transom is the housing of the SQR-19 TACTASS towed array.

▼ The Ticonderoga, propelled by gas turbines, are equipped with exhaust filters to reduce temperatures and radar signatures. Pictured is the Hue City, CG 66 cruiser entering port.

envisaged. Instead, two consortia were formed, Blue Team and Gold Team, which are carrying out projects with both similarities and differences.

The current plan seems to be for a ship of more than 200 m in length, armed with between 64 and 128 VLS, and one or two 155 mm guns which will fire Rocket Assisted Projectiles (RAP) guided by GPS, with a range of up to 100 km or more. Both its displacement and the caliber of artillery employed mean it should be considered as a cruiser, possibly a heavy cruiser.
The first ship is forecast to enter service towards 2008 and the cost is estimated at 650 million dollars per ship at present, although this will probably rise. In total, 32 ships, to be delivered over 10 years, are planned. Each ship will have an active military life of about 35 years.

RUSSIAN
CRUISERS

The Russian navy is the only one to currently maintain in action large surface ships whose armament is designed to attack enemy ships, especially aircraft carriers.

The anti-aircraft carrier strategy

The death of Stalin in March 1953 and the entry into service of the great American attack aircraft carriers during the 1950s brought about changes in the philosophy and strategy of the Soviet Navy. This was accentuated when the first real SSM anti-ship missiles, the SS-N-2 Styx became available. These powerful new weapons were deployed on over 100 rapid missile launches of the Komar and Osa classes, whose efficacy was demonstrated in 1967, with the sinking of the Israeli destroyer Eilath by a Komar ceded to Egypt. Also important was the first shooting down of an anti-ship missile by an anti-missile missile in Vietnam in 1972, when a SAM Terrier, fired from the Sterett DLG-31, destroyed an SS-N-2 launched from a North Vietnamese Komar launch.

The anti-submarine strategy

During the same era, the US Navy's new fleet of submarines armed with Polaris missiles became operational, with missiles aimed at the USSR.

The Russians, at first, designed and constructed hybrids of the Moskwa class named Protivolodochny Kreyser or anti-submarine cruisers, whose flight deck could house up to 14 ASW Ka-25 Hormone helicopters, ships similar to Western helicopter-carrying cruisers like the Italian Andrea Doria and Vittorio Veneto or the French Jeanne d'Arc. In May 1975, the Kiev, the first ship of its class equipped with SS-N-12 Sandbox anti-ship missiles (AsuW) with nuclear warhead capacity, and Ka Hormone helicopters, entered service.

The latest Russian cruisers

In July 1980, it was revealed that the Soviet fleet had received a large cruiser, the Kirov, the first nuclear surface ship in the Russian combat fleet with a displacement and measurements comparable to the battleships and cruisers of the two World Wars. More ships followed, the Frunze in 1983, the Kalinin in 1988 and the Pyotr Velikiy (ex Yuri Andropov) in 1995. Their official name is Reketny Kreyser or missile cruiser.

With the same denomination, another new class of ship the Slava entered service. Five were planned, the Slava, Marshal Ustinov, Chevrona Ukraina, Admiral Lobov and another which was cancelled in 1990. Of the four Kirov, only two, the Pyotr Velikiy and Admiral Nakhimov (ex Kalinin) are currently active. The other two, the Admiral Ushakov (ex Kirov) and

▼ *The Slava's offensive weaponry includes 16 Chelomey SS-N-12 Sandbox anti-ship missiles (550 km range at 1.7 Mach, with active and intertial radar guidance), with nuclear (350kt) or HE(1,000 kg) warheads, mounted two-by-two with four launchers on each side. The electronics are excellent, with three-dimensional air-search Top Pair radar in the stern, which detects large targets at 366 km and targets as small as two square meters at 183 km, and 3D Top Steer air and surface search radar mounted on top of the bridge.*

▶ *The rivalry between two power blocs, such a characteristic of the recent past, led to the development of very powerful warships designed to destroy naval and land-based targets with guns and missiles.*

Admiral Lazarev (ex Frunze) are attached to the reserves of the Northern and Pacific fleets. The names of the Slava class ships were also changed to Moskva (ex Slava), Marshall Ustinov, Varyag (ex Chernova Ukraina) and Admiral Lobov (ex Ukraina), the last of which is slowly being completed and may well be sold to a foreign power.

The Kirov

These heavy cruisers are the largest warships to be built since WW2, except for aircraft carriers, and are propelled by a mixed Combined Nuclear and Steam (CONAS) system, consisting of two pressurized water reactors producing steam that is reheated in conventional petrol-burning boilers.

Their silhouette is blocky and powerful, with considerable differences between each ship, the result of experience, with resulting variations in performance.

The military potential of these ships is based on their 20 ASuW Chelomney SS-N-19 Shipwreck supersonic missiles (1.6 Mach) which can be fitted with nuclear warheads. They have a low flight profile (sea-skimming) and are basically a modification of the SS-12-N contained in vertical silos in the forecastle. Forward of these are twelve eight-bay vertical silos containing SAM SA-N-6 Grumble air defense missiles which form part of the AEGIS defense system and are also supersonic, with nuclear warhead capabilities. The range of SAM missiles is completed by two launching ramps containing 40 SA-N-4 Gekko point defense missiles with a speed of Mach 2.5 and 128 SA-N-9 Gauntlet missiles. The range of missiles is completed by six mixed batteries of 8 missiles and 2 30mm CADS-N-1 guns and SS-N-15 Starfish ASW, each with a

19

torpedo with conventional or nuclear warheads and 10 533mm torpedo launchers in batteries of 5, which can launch various torpedoes and even SS-N-15 missiles.

The electronic sensors are composed of 3D Top Pair air search radar,Top Plate air-surface radar, Palm Frond navigation, Cross Sword, Top Dome, Tomb Stone, Pop Ground; Kite Screech and Hot Flash launch control systems, Flyscreen B, IFF Salt Pod A and B and Tacan Round House air control, Tin Man, Punch Bowl SATCOM, Low Ball SATNAV arms control and Bell Crown and Bell Push data links, Horse Jaw and VDS Horse Tail systems. ESM/ECM Foot Ball, Wine Flask, Bell Bash, Bell Nip, Half Cup electronic warfare systems, PK2 150 mm decoy launchers and towable torpedoes.

The Slava

The Slava are propelled by 6 COGAG gas turbines, 2 for cruising speeds and 4 more for maximum speed and two propellers, with a total power of 108,000 CV; 32 knots and an autonomy of 2,500 miles at 30 knots or 15,000 at 7 knots The displacement is 11,200 tons fully loaded.

They are armed with SSM/ASuW SS-N-12, SAM/AAW SA-N-6 and SA-N-4 missiles, ASW RBU-6000 rocket launchers, a twin-tower 130/70 mm gun, an AK 130 and 6 batteries of CIWS AK 650.

The Slava are well-protected, with 64 SA-N-6 anti-air/anti-missile missiles (in an eight-battery VLS) and 40 SA-N-4 with twin retractable launchers. The SA-N-6 is an ultrasupersonic missile (Mach 6) with nuclear or HE capabilities, a range of 80 km and a maximum altitude of 30,000 m. The stern housed the Ka-27 Helix helicopter hangar and, above it, the Top Dome radar director/missile illuminator for SA-N-6 missiles.

Technical Characteristics

Performance:	Kirov	Slava
Class/number	Kirov (4)	Slava (4)
Delivery	1988/1998	1982/1986/1989
Length/beam/draught	252x28.9x9.1	186.4x20.8x20.4
Displacement	24,300 tons	11,490 tons
Propulsion	CONAS	COGAG
Engines	GT3A-688 Turbines	M-70 Turbines
Power	140,000 CV	88,000 CV
Speed/range	30 knots 14,000/30	32 knots 7,500/15
Weapon systems:	20 SSM SS-N-19	15 SSM SS-N-12
	40 SAM SA-N-4	64 SAM SA-N-6
	96 SAM SA-N-6	40 SAM SA-N-4
	128 SAM SA-N-9	2 guns 130/70
	6 CIWS CADS-N1	6 CIWS AKA 650
	ASW SS-N-15	10 TL 533 mm
	2 guns 130/70	2 ASW RBU 6000
	10 TL 533 mm	mortars
	1 ASW RBU 12000 mortar	
	2 ASW RBU 1000 mortars	

MEDIUM
ESCORTS

The appearance of the automobile torpedo, with the ability to sink large ships during the last quarter of the XIX century, signaled a new era.

The birth of two new ships

The appearance of the torpedo revolutionized naval thinking, with new ideas like those of the French "jeune école" which forecast the practical disappearance of the great battleships, helpless against the threat of torpedoes. It was also thought that the torpedo boats, cheap, agile, effective and available to any navy would be the wave of the future.

As has often happened, one ship gave its name to a whole class. Thus, the heirs of the Destroyer were called destroyers (Zerstörer in German) or torpedo fighters. These new ships were armed with rapid-fire guns and torpedo launchers and their speed allowed them to rival and even

exceed the torpedo boats. They had ocean-going capacity and displacement, although life for the crew was hard

A long evolution

The evolution of the destroyer passed from the 380 tons and 58.7 m length of the Destroyer to the 9,000 tons and 155 m length of the Oscar Austin (Arleigh A. Burke flight IIA). As a result, the capacity considered 50 years ago as commensurate with a cruiser would today qualify only as a destroyer.

After the Second World War, the role of the destroyer was replaced in some duties by the frigate, whose performance increased, and today, the basic differences between

the two categories are few. The number of destroyers has been reduced from 815 in 1956 to 206 in 1998.

A doubtful classification

The performance and capacity of current destroyers are similar to those of other categories, making it difficult to distinguish between a destroyer and a frigate, with the displacement and maximum speed marking the difference.

Not all countries have preserved the denomination of destroyer, with some preferring the term multi-mission frigate. The markings D or F on a ship's side are also not definitive, as the signs are not universally used.

The missions carried out by medium-sized escort vessels involve anti-submarine, anti-aircraft and anti-surface warfare, so they are usually multi-purpose ships that combine various military capabilities.

The Combat Information Centre (CIC) on a modern warship is the place where specialists working at a series of consoles directing the systems and sensors control all military activities.

Technical Characteristics

Performance:	Destroyer	Mohawk	Fletcher
Year/country	1887/Spain	1907/ United Kingdom	1942/USA
Displacement	380 tons	865 tons	2.750 tons
Length/beam/draught	58.7x7.6x2.4	83.8x7.5x4.7	115x12x3.5
Engines	Alternating	Steam turbines	Steam turbines
Power	3,800 CV	14,500 CV	60,000 CV
Propellers	2	3	2
Speed/range	22.5-2,000/cruise speed	34-2,350/15 knots	35-6,000/15 knots
Crew	60	50	350
Weaponry:	1 gun 90 mm; 4 57 Nordenfeldt; 2 37 Hotchkiss ; 3 457 mm torpedo launchers	3 rapid-fire 76/40 mm guns; 2 457 mm torpedo launchers	5 127 mm guns; 6 40/60 mm; 10 20 mm; 10 533 mm torpedo launchers; 2 LC depthcharges; 6 LC mortars

The US Navy is one of the few with destroyers currently in service.

Modern American destroyers

Before WW2 the USA laid the foundations of the Two Ocean Fleet, the largest and most impor-
tant fleet of destroyers. The Fletcher, DD 445 class was succeeded by the Allen M.Sumner,
DD 692, class, and this, in turn, by the Gearing, DD 710 class, of which the last built was the
Meredith, DD 890 which entered service on the last day of 1945.

The postwar period

Of the 481 ships of these three classes, more than 300 were still in service in the 1960s fulfilling
various missions, reconverted or armed with missiles. Some Sumner and Gearing class ships were
modernized, prolonging their life by more than a decade. A large number finished their life serving
in allied navies such as Korea, Spain, Greece, Mexico, Taiwan and Turkey.

The DDG

During the 1970s the Charles F.Adams destroyers began to enter service, initiating the new
DDG series incorporating SAM anti-air missiles.
In addition, the USA financed the construction of three ships for Germany and two for

25

Australia. The original series was decommissioned after 1990, with some ships being ceded to the Greek fleet in 1992 (Kimon, Nearchos, Fornion and Themistocles).

The Spruance

The Spruance series were conceived at the end of the 1960s to replace the FRAM, although in practice, they also replaced the Forrest Sherman.

The flagship was delivered in 1975 and the last, the Hayler, DD 997, in 1983. Construction of the 31 ships involved two innovative procedures; total welded modular construction and the building of all ships in the same dockyard, thus, lowering costs by mass production.

Wartime operations

In principal, the DDG were large-capacity destroyers which, due to the availability of the Sea Sparrow, Harpoon and Tomahawk were converted into destroyers with anti-air and later anti-ship missile capabilities, and were the only destroyers with ground-attack capacities, as shown during Operation Desert Storm when they launched Tomahawk missiles (Caron/2; Fife/60; Leftwich/8; Paul F.Foster/40 and Spruance/2) against Iraq and in 1993 when the Caron, Hewitt, Stump and Peterson also launched missiles.

Weaponry

Originally, their weaponry comprised two 127/ 54 mm Mk 45 guns in one automatic turret, an

A Tomahawk being fired from the aft vertical launcher. Similarly sized ships in service with other western countries do not have this ability to attack land-based targets.

eight-barrel launcher for ASROC anti-ship missiles and ASW torpedoes. When they entered service they were equipped with CIWS anti-missile missiles and Sea Sparrow missiles.

The Harpoon missile has always been loaded in lots of four, usually housed amidships. For Tomahawk missiles, some ships, after 1982 were equipped with two four-barrel ABL (Armored Box Launcher) in the forecastle, one to each side of the ASROC launcher. In 1987 they were replaced by a 61-well VLS Mk 41 which in some cases also replaced the Sea Sparrow launchers.

The Kidd

In 1973 the Iranian government ordered AAW destroyers, based on the Spruance class. Finally, the ships were bought by the US Navy after the fall of the Shah's regime in 1979, to avoid them falling into the hands of the new Islamic government. They remained in service until 1999 and in 2001 were offered to Taiwan. The coste of reactivating them is estimated at 760.8 million dollars, with the first delivery scheduled in 2004 and the last in 2006.

The Arleigh A. Burke

The Arleigh A. Burke were conceived as replacements for the Charles F. Adams and Coontz classes. The Arleigh A. Burke and Oscar Austin series differed in their weaponry and other characteristics.

Forty-nine Burke were planned during the Carter administration, a figure increased during the

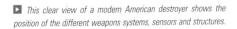 The shape of the 'Arleigh Burke' destroyers is one of the most advanced and they incorporate design modifications and equipment to make them harder for enemy radars to detect.

▶ This clear view of a modern American destroyer shows the position of the different weapons systems, sensors and structures.

Reagan years. However, their cost of around 1 billion dollars per ship reduced expectations. Flight I and II, Flight IIA (Oscar Austin) were built and entered service from 2000 onwards. The Burke had three special characteristics. They were the first ships equipped with stealth technology, they had a length/beam ratio much lesser than normal, and they were the first to use the concept of NBC (nuclear/biologic/chemical) substructures, which converts them into hermetically sealed spaces, provided with accesses through the double doors which form an airlock. They were also the first destroyers to use multi-role SPY-1DK phase-panel sensors.

▼ *The potential of modern surface warships has been increased by their ability to embark sophisticated helicopters fitted with highly capable sensors and systems, such as this Sea Hawk.*

Characteristics Compared

Performance:	Spruance	Kidd	Burke	Oscar Austin
Class/number	Spruance (31)	Kidd (4)	Arleigh A.Burke (28)	Oscar Austin (23)
Delivery	1975/1983	1981/1982	1991/1999	2000/2006
Length/beam/draught	172x16.8x8.8	172x16.8x10	153.8x20.4x10	155.3x20.4x9.9
Desplacement	8,280 tons	9,574 tons	8,422/9,033 tons	9,238 tons
Propulsion	Gas turbines	Gas turbines	Gas turbines	Gas turbines
Engines	LM 2500 (4)	LM 2500 (4)	LM 2500 (4)	LM 2500/30 (4)
Power	86,000 CV	86,000 CV	105,000 CV	105,000 CV
Speed/range	32.5-6,000/20	30-6,000/20	32-4,400/20	32-4,400/20
Weaponry:	Tomahawk/ASROC (61)/VLS	Harpoon (8)	Tomahawk/ASROC/ Standard (90)	Tomahawk/ASROC/ Standard (96)
	Sea Sparrow (8)	Standard SM-2MR (52)	Harpoon (8)	Harpoon (8)
	Harpoon (8)	ASROC (16)	1 127/54 mm ERGM Gun	1 127/54 mm ERGM Gun
	RAM	2 127/54 mm	2 CIWS Vulcan Phalanx	2 CIWS Vulcan Phalanx
	2 127/54 mm Gun	2 CIWS Vulcan Phalanx	2xIII LT/ASW 324 mm	2xIII LT/ASW 324 mm
	2 CIWS Vulcan Phalanx	4 12.7 mm Machine Guns		
	4 12.7 mm Machine Guns	2xIII LT/ASW 324 mm		
	2xIII LT/ASW 324 mm	1 LAMPS III Helicopters		
	2 LAMPS III Helicopters			

RUSSIAN
DESTROYERS

Russia has influence in four different seas and thus needs a large and effective fleet.

From the Skoryi to the Kashin

At the end of WW2, Stalin applied part of the USSR's industrial potential to the construction of a large naval fleet.

The first destroyer built during the Cold War was the Skoryi. Between 1949 and 1954, 72 ships were built. The power units of low pressure boilers and turbines at low temperatures were not modern, the electronic equipment had only limited air-search capacity and the sonar was not effective against the latest nuclear submarines.

The Skoryi were replaced by the Kotlin (with anti-air, radar fire-controll weaponry), the Kildin (armed with anti-ship SS-N-1missiles), the Krupny (with greater missile capacity), the Kynda (officially cruisers), the Kanin (1961-1963) and the Kashin (1962-1973, powered by gas turbines).

New ships

The most important destroyers in the current Russian fleet appeared during the 1980s, and were named the Sovremenny (with anti-ship capabilities) and the Udaloy, conceived for anti-submarine warfare.

The Sovremenny

The Sovremenny had a forecastle which reached the bridge, a traditional weapons distribution with a double tower of 130/70 mm guns and a double ramp for Gadfly missiles on the

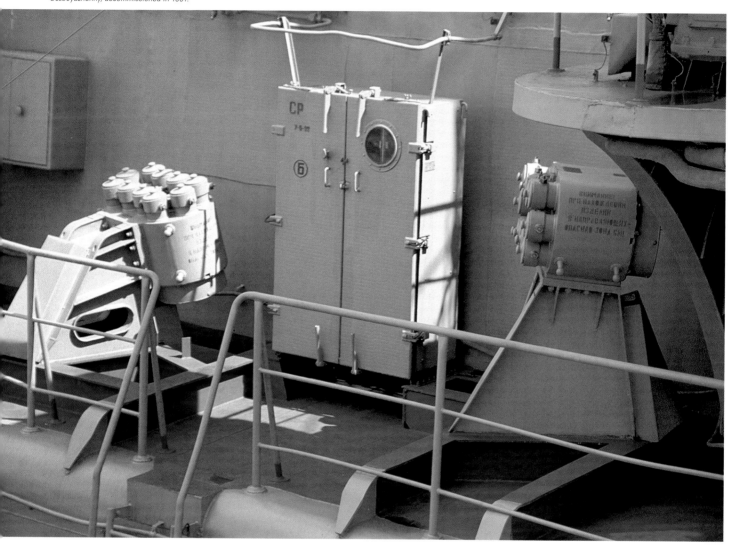

bow and stern and on either side of the bridge, and two four-barreled SSM Sunburn missile launchers.

Weaponry

The weaponry included SS-N-22 Sunburn anti-ship missiles, SA-N-7 Gadfly or SA-N-17 (in later ships) anti-air/anti-missile missiles and 130/70 mm anti-ship/anti-air and AK-630 anti-missile guns. In addition it was equipped with anti-submarine RBU 1.000 torpedo launchers, mines and a Ka-25 Hormone B helicopter for missile guidance.

Electronics

The electronic sensors include 3-D Top Plate (or Strut Pair) air-search radar; Palm Frond ground-search radar; Cross Sword fire-control radar; Eye Bowl; Kite Screech (for the 100 mm guns) and Bass Tilt; Horse Jaw and VDS Horse Tail sonar; Foot Ball, Bell Shroud and Bell Squat electronic warfare systems; two PK-2 and eight PK-10 decoy launchers and noise-reduction systems.

Characteristics

Not all the series projected was completed. The ships should have a substantial radar

signature, due to the mass and volume of the superstructures and because no system to reduce the radar signature was used in the hull.

The Udaloy

The Sovremenny were considered as destroyers with some anti-submarine capabilities, while the Udaloy class, somewhat larger, are true anti-submarine ships with some AsuW capabilites. They are powered by COGAG (125.000 CV) gas turbines on two propellers and the raised deck is oriented more to the stern.

The Sovremenny are powered by traditional steam turbines – two GTZA-674 and four KVN boilers. The photo shows the Bespekoiny.

Weaponry

The Udaloy are equipped with eight SS-N-14 Silex ASW missiles, two Ka-27 Helix A helicopters, two RBU-6000 rocket launchers and two four-barrel 533 mm torpedo launchers, 64 SA-N-9 anti-air/anti-missile missiles and four CIWS Ak-630 guns. In addition, there are two multipurpose 100/59mm anti-ship/anti-air guns with simple mounts and 30 mines.

Electronics

The electronic sensors include 3-D Top Plate (or Strut Pair) air-search radar; Palm Frond ground-search radar; Cross Sword fire-control radar; Eye Bowl; Kite Screech (for the 100 mm guns) and Bass Tilt; Horse Jaw and VDS Horse Tail sonar; Foot Ball, Bell Shroud and Bell Squat electronic warfare systems; two PK-2 and eight PK-10 decoy launchers and noise-reduction systems.

The Type 1155.1

There is a second model in the Udaloy class with different weaponry. The type 1155.1 has eight SSM SS-N-22 Sunburn missiles, 64 SA-N-9 Gauntlet missiles, ASW SS-N-15 Starfish missiles, two CADS-N-1mixed missile/gun systems, two 130/70 guns in double formation, two ASW RBU 6.000 mortars and eight 533 mm torpedo launchers in two banks of four. Only the Admiral Chabanenko is in service; the Admiral Basisty was scrapped in 1994 and the Admiral Kucherov was not begun.

■ Russian warships have evolved and become very versatile and highly capable, although still considerably short of western standards. Their price makes them attractive military purchases.

■ The high forecastle of the Udaloy means they perform well in rough seas. The forward VLS are located on the foredeck, together with some of the SAM SA-N-9 Gauntlet missiles.

Characteristics Compared

Performance:	Sovremenny	Udaloy	Udaloy II
Class/number	Sovremenny (19)	Udaloy (10)	Udaloy II (1)
Delivery	1985/2000	1983/1991	1995
Length/beam/draught	156x17.3x6.5	164x19.3x7.5	164x19.3x7.5
Desplacement	7,940 tons	8,500 tons	8,900 tons
Propulsion	KVN Steam Boilers	COGAG	COGAG
Engines	GTZA-674 Turbines	Gas Turbines	Gas Turbines
Power	99,500 CV	69,100 CV	72,800 CV
Speed/range	32-14,000/14	29-7,700/18	28-4,000/18
Weaponry:	8 SSM SS-N-22 Sunburn	64 SAM SA-N-9 Gauntlet	8 SSM SS-N-22 Sunburn
	44 SAM SA-N-7/12/17	8 ASW SA-N-14 Silex	64 SAM SA-N-9 Gauntlet
	2xII 130/70 mm Guns	2xI 100/59 mm Guns	ASW SS-N-15 Starfish
	4xVI CIWS AK-630, 30 mm	4xVI CIWS AK-630, 30 mm	2 CADS-N-1 (8 SA-N-11+2 AK-630)
	2xII 533 mm Torpedo Launchers	2xIV 533 mm Torpedo Launchers	1xII 130/70 mm Guns
	2xVI ASW RBU	2xXII ASW RBU	2xIV 533 mm Torpedo Launchers
	1000 Mortars	6000 Mortars	2xXII ASW RBU
	Max 40 mines	Max 26 mines	6000 Mortars

◀ The ships from the third batch are 16 m longer, with a bigger forecastle and raking stern. Construction was delayed to allow the lessons learned from the Falklands War to be applied. Pictured is the Manchester, D-95.

▶ This photo of the Glasgow, D-88 shows the domes of the Type 42 ships, housing two Marconi 9.091 fire-control radars operating in I/J bands.

The United Kingdom, France and Italy are the European countries whose navies currently possess conventional destroyers.

The Type 42

When the aircraft-carrier production program was cancelled in 1966, the Royal Navy built the Type 42 destroyers as it was considered essential to have squadron escorts with air-defense capacities.

Different types

Five ships took part in the Falklands War, of which the Sheffield and Coventry were sunk and the Glasgow damaged. Another group of ships has a larger displacement, the deck is longer and wider and a strip has been added to port and starboard to widen the passage along the superstructure.

Propulsion and weaponry

The Type 42 are powered by gas turbines (COGOG) and their weaponry, besides the Sea Dart, comprises a 114/55 mm Mk-8 gun, light guns (plus two CIWS Vulcan Phalanx), anti-submarine torpedoes and /or a Lynx helicopter. It is projected to replace the Type 42 with the Type 45 /Horizon from 2007 onwards.

The Georges Leygues/Cassard

The French F-70 destroyers were replacements for the Surcouf (class T-47) and Duperré (class T-53), decommissioned during the 1980s. The class is composed of one type ASW, the Georges Leygues and another AAW the Cassard.

ASW ships

The class comprises the Georges Leygues, Dupleix, Montcalm, Jean de Vienne, Primaugue, La Motte-Picquet and Latouche-Treville. They have CODOG propulsion (two RR Olympus TM3B turbines and two diesel SEMT-Pielstick 16 PA6 V280), with a top speed of 30 knots (21 with diesel), a range of 8,500 miles at 18 knots (with diesel) or 2,500 miles at 28 knots (with turbines).

Modernization plan

The ships are currently undergoing an OP3A (Opération Amélioration Autodéfense Antimissiles) upgrading which will improve the weapons systems (two six-battery SAM

Matra Sadral launchers, ASW Matra/Bae Milas missiles and two Breda-Mauser 30 mm guns). In addition, a command post will be added over the bridge. The rest of the weaponry includes SSM Exocet missiles; a battery of eight SAM Crotale Naval supersonic missiles, a 100/55 mm mod 68 CADAM automatic multipurpose gun, two Oerlikon 20 mm guns, four 12.7 mm machine guns, ASW torpedoes and a Lynx helicopter.

AAW ships

In 1988 and 1991, the French navy received the destroyers Cassard and Jean Bart, conceived for anti-air/ anti-missile warfare. They were built on F-70 ASW hulls and propelled with diesel engines which gave sufficient range and speed to serve as escorts to aircraft-carrier groups, including nuclear ones.

The Luigi Durand de la Penne

In the 1980s, Italy undertook the construction of modern destroyers, which were delivered beginning in 1992, receiving the names of war heroes, Luigi Durand de la penne and Francesco Mimbell. Delivery was delayed by the Italian navy due to excessive noise in the engines.

Tried and tested

Every inch of the ships are used for some installation. Built of steel alloys and protected with Kevlar in strategic areas, they have a Prairie noise-reduction system.
They use a CODOG propulsion system on two shafts with variable pitch propellers. The weaponry comprises SSM Teseo Mk 2 missiles, ASW Milas missiles, 40 SAM Standard SM-1MR, 16 SAM Aspide, a 127/54 mm gun, three OTO-Melara 76/62 mm Super Rapid guns, six ASW 324 mm torpedo launchers and two AB-212 ASW helicopters. The ships can also operate with the SH-3D Sea King and with the new EH-101 Merlin.

Type 45

The Type 45 ships result from the failure of the NFR-90 unified frigate project for the European NATO countries. The first is scheduled to enter service in 2007.

The ships are being built by BAE Systems. Equipped with PAAMS (Principal Anti-Air Missile System), they will be anti-air destroyers projected to remain active until 2040. Propulsion is provided by integrated electric Rolls Royce WR 21; two conventional propeller shafts and variable pitch propellers. They have a displacement of over 7,000 tons, a top speed of 29 knots, and a range of 7,000 miles at 18 knots. The weaponry includes a 114/55 mm gun, two 30mm guns and two CIWS Vulcan Phalanx systems, Aster 15, Aster 30 and Harpoon missiles.

Horizon

The Horizon Program is a joint venture between France and Italy. The ships are scheduled to enter service between 2006 and 2009.

The displacement will be 6,700 tons fully loaded, with a maximum length of 150.6 m, a beam of 19.9m and a draught of 4.8m excluding domes. They will use a CODOG propulsion system with two LM gas turbines and two French SEMT-Pielstick diesel turbines. The maximum speed will be 29 knots, with a range of 7,000 miles at 18 knots.

The Cassard are adapted for AAW, – the photo shows the Cassard, D-614 – and are equipped with a 3D Thomson CSF DRBJ 11B air-seach radar, with a range of 366 km, located on top of the stern superstructure under a protective dome.

▶ The new generation Type 45 destroyers will be the most modern in the Royal Navy. Their armament, including a flight deck for heavy helicopters, is much stronger than that of the Type 42 currently in service.

Characteristics Compared

Performance:	Type 42/I	Type 42/II	Type 42/III	G-Leygues	Cassard	De la Penne
Class/ number	Birmingham (6)	Exeter (4)	Manchester (4)	Georges L.(7)	Cassard (2)	Luigi Durand de la Penne (2)
Delivery	1976/1979	1980/1982	1982/1985	1979/1990	1988/1991	1993
Length/beam/draught	125x14.3x5.8	125x14.3x5.8	141x14.9x5.8	139x14x5.7	138x14x6.5	148x16x1x8.6
Displacement	4,100 tons	4,100 tons	4,675 tons	4,580 tons	4,730 tons	5,400 tons
Propulsion	COGOG	COGOG	COGOG	CODOG	Diesel	COGOG
Engines	Olympus TM3B (2) Tyne RM1C (2)	Olympus TM3B (2) Tyne RM1C (2)	Olympus TM3B (2) Tyne RM1C (2)	Olympus TM3B SEMT-Pielstick (2)	SEMT-Pielstick (4)	Fiat/LM 2500 (2) GMT BL 230.20 (2)
Power	50,000/9,900	50,000/9,900	43,000/10,680	46,200/12,800	43,200	54,000/12,600
Speed/range	29-4,000/18	29-4,000/18	>30-4,000/18	30-21-8,500/18	29.5-4,800/24	31-21-7,000/18
Weaponry:	22 SAM Sea Dart 1 114/55 mm Mk 8 Gun 2xVI CIWS Vulcan Phalanx Various 20 mm 6 TL ASW 324 mm (2xIII) 1 Lynx Helicopter	22 SAM Sea Dart 1 114/55 mm Mk 8 Gun 2xVI CIWS Vulcan Phalanx Various 20 mm 6 TL ASW 324 mm (2xIII) 1 Lynx Helicopter	22 SAM Sea Dart 1 114/55 mm Mk 8 Gun 2xVI CIWS Vulcan Phalanx Various 20 mm 6 TL ASW 324 mm (2xIII) 1 Lynx Helicopter	1 SAM/CIWS Crotale Naval 2 CIWS Simbad or Sadral 1 100/55 Mod. 8 Gun Various 30 and/ or 20 mm + 12.7 mm TL ASW 324 mm 2 Lynx Helicopters	8 SSM Exocet 40 SAM Standard SM-1MR 2 CIWS Sadral 1 100/55 Mod. 8 Gun 2 Oerlikon 20 mm + 12.7 mm 2 TL ASW 324 mm 1 AS 565MA Panther Helicopters	8 SSM Matra Teseo Mk 2 40 SAM Standard SM-1MR 16 DPMS Aspide 1 127/54 mm Gun 3 76/62 mm(3xI) Guns 6 TL ASW 324 mm (2xIII) 2 AB-212 Helicopters

OTHER
DESTROYERS

Current destroyers or medium escorts include various models, some of which are now obsolete.

The Iroquois

In 1968, Canada ordered the DDH-280 or Tribal class destroyers, with the projected names of Iroquois, Huron, Athabaskan and Algonquin.

Before and after

The first version was armed with two four-battery SAM Sea Sparrow launchers, fixed on both sides of the superstructure in front of the bridge; an Italian OTO-Melara 127/54 mm gun, six ASW 324 mm torpedo launchers in banks of three with Honeywell Mk 46 torpedoes and a triple ASW Limbo Mk 10 launcher, as well as two CH-124A Sea King helicopters. Power was provided by gas turbines (COGOG).

The TRUMP modification

Between 1987 and 1995 the ships underwent a TRUMP (TRibal class Update and Modernization Project) upgrade. The gun was replaced by a OTO-Melara 76/62 mm more elevated in the 02 deck, and the forecastle deck was occupied by a VLS Mk 41 with SAM Standard SM-2MR Block III missiles; a CIWS Vulcan Phalanx was sited on the cover of the hangar, the TL ASW 324 mm reamained and the Limbo mortar was removed.

The sensors became mainly Signaal, with the antenna of the SPQ-502 air-search radar sited on the roof of the bridge.

The Japonese MSDF

After WW2, the rise of communism in Asia led Japan to increase the size of its so-called "self-defense" navy, with the agreement of the Allied powers. Currently, Japan has one of the largest navies in the world consisting of some 140 modern ships (18 SSK, 44 DD/DDG,

▼ *The Iroquois with the Westinghouse SQS-510 VDS sonar trawled array, suspended on the aft superstructure near the transom stern.*

10 FF/FFG, 13 amphibian vessels, 34 MCMV and 24 auxiliary ships) with about 12 more scheduled to be delivered before 2010. In addition, the Japanese Maritime Safety Agency possesses about 500 vessels of various sizes.

The Kongo

Japan's most modern ships are the Kongo destroyers which entered service between 1993 and 1998, and, like the US Navy ships employ the AEGIS system.

Shared technology

The Kongo are similar in displacement and weaponry to the Arleigh A.Burke class ships. The weaponry includes two VLS batteries for SAM and ASW missiles, SSM Harpoon anti-ship missiles, ASROC anti-submarine missiles, ASW Honeywell Mk 46 mod. 5 Neartip torpedoes and Seahawk/ SH-60 J helicopters. The artillery is composed of an OTO-Melarae 127/54 mm gun and two Vulcan Phalanx CIWS.

The Takanami

Japan is now building the new Takanami class ships, which are a modification of the Murasame. Changes include more missiles, with improvements in the missile firing systems and a new sonar. They will enter service in 2003 (2), 2004, 2005 and 2006.

The Takanami have a displacement of 5,150 tons fully loaded, and are armed with 32 VLS, 8 SSM-1B Mitsubishi, 1 Otobreda 127/54 gun, 2 CIWS Vulcan Phalanx and TL ASW 324 m and a Mitsubishi/Sikorsky SH-60 helicopter.

American Mk45 gun on automatic fire. Its 127mm shells can hit targets more than fifty kilometres away, although doing so requires guidance in the terminal flight phase.

The Marasesti

Rumania does not have a large fleet, but does possess a ship with a marked personality, the Marasesti destroyer. Projected to be built with Soviet help, it was conceived as a multi-role destroyer with SSM and ASW, with CODAG propulsion.

Inherited problems

The keel was laid down in 1979 and the hull launched in 1981. The project had to be modified for economic and technical reasons. The two gas turbines could not be delivered on time and a diesel CODAD propulsion system was used instead.

Unusual propulsion

The propulsion system is German, with four three-blade propellers; two interior reversible pitch propellers in the stern used for cruising and maneuvering and two fixed exterior propellers in the bow. Control is through two semi-compensated rudders.

Weaponry and electronics

The weaponry includes eight SS-N-2 C Styx missiles, which were originally located on the first deck in double batteries and ASW morters on the superstructure. However, problems of listing, meant the centre of gravity had to be lowered and the missiles were placed on a lower deck, the mortars on a higher one and the masts were shortened.

▶ The RBU 6.000 anti-submarine rocket launchers fire projectiles with a warhead of 31 kg of HE with a range of 6 km.

▼ The Canadian Iroquois destroyers, such as the Algonquin, DDG-283 pictured here, have been upgraded by the TRUMP modernization, prolonging their active life.

Characteristics Compared

Performance:	Iroquois	Kongo	Takanami	Marasesti
Class/number	Iroquois (4)	Kongo (4+2)	Takanami (4)	Marasesti (1)
Delivery	1972/1973	1993/1998	2003/2006	1985
Length/beam/draught	130x15.2x6.6	161x21x10	171x17.4x5.3	145x14.8x7
Displacement	5,100 tons	9,485 tons	5,150 tons	5,790 tons
Propulsion	COGOG	COGAG	COGAG	CODAD
Engines	Pratt & Whitney FT4 Allison 570-KF A2	LM 2500	LM 2500+Spey SM1C	diesels
Power	50,000/12,700 CV	102,160 CV	84,630 CV	32,000 CV
Speed/range	27/15-4,500/15	30-4,500/20	30	27
Weaponry:	29 SAM Standard SM-2MR III 1 OTO Melara 76/62 mm Gun 1 CIWS Vulcan Phalanx 6 TL ASW 324 mm (2xIII) 2 CH-124 Sea King Helicopters	8 SSM Harpoon 90 SAM/ASW Standard/ ASROC 1 OTO Melara 127/54 mm Gun 2 CIWS Vulcan Phalanx 6 TL ASW 324 mm (2xIII) 1 Helicopter (with hangar in the modified series)	8 SSM-1B Mitsubishi 32 SAM/ASW Sea Sparrow/ASROC 1 Otobreda 127/54 mm Gun 2 CIWS Vulcan Phalanx 6 TL ASW 324 mm (2xIII) 1 Helicopter	8 SSM SS-N-2 C Styx 4 76/60 mm Guns 4 CIWS AK-630 6 TL 533 mm 2 ASW RBU 6000 Mortars 2 Alouette Helicopters

LIGHT ESCORTS

◀ Modern warships' potential means that they can also carry out tasks designated as auxiliary. Here a warship is launching remote-controlled aircraft used in air defence exercises.

▶ The German frigate F-208 Niedersachsen was the second of the 'Bremen' class to commission, in 1982. She is very powerful and carries five missile launchers.

The frigate, a versatile ship whose origins lie in the days of sail, is a confusing denomination.

A rapid change

During WW2, the frigate developed as a ship with a capacity lesser than a destroyer and greater than a corvette, ideal for anti-submarine warfare and the protection of merchant convoys.

These tasks meant great speed was not necessary, as the submarines of the time usually could not reach sustained speeds of 4-6 knots underwater, a similar speed to that of a convoy crossing the Atlantic.

As it was more rapid and cheaper and less complicated to build, the frigate was an ideal ship to escort convoys, especially in the fight against German U-boats.

The frigate in the postwar period

The frigate of these times had a displacement of around 1,000 tons and a maximum speed of around 20 knots Often powered by old-fashioned steam engines, new military demands led to rapid changes. At the end of WW2 and in the years after the Korean War, the denomination of frigate included a group of ships with similar tasks but very different origins,

including old and converted destroyers, and new, purpose-built ships, which in the USA received the name of destroyer escorts.

The USA financed the construction of anti-submarine boats for France (the classs Le Normand and Le Corse, which received American designations – OF-1.007 / 1.013 and OF-1.016 / 1.019-), Italy (the Castore) and Portugal (the Pero Escobar). The US Navy itself began construction of various series with the denomination of OF (García, Bronstein classes, etc.), and others such as the Brooke (DEG as it incorporated missiles), which, after 1969, became the Knox Class. All these ships were redesignated as frigates from 1975.

From 1977 onwards, the Oliver H. Perry class became operational. Originally designated PF (Patrol Frigate), and later as FFG, these ships were designed as tanker escorts as part of the anti-SLOC (Sea Line Of Communications) strategy, in which war with the USSR was believed inevitable. Currently, there are about 450 fighting ships designated as frigates, with about 25 still to enter service. Some will be decommissioned and others sold.

Today's frigate usually has a displacement of between 3,000 and 6,000 tons fully loaded, with combined propulsion (mainly CODOG or COGAG) and a range of between 4,000 and 6,000 miles at speeds of between 15 and 20 knots The missile load includes SAM, ASW and ASuW, with light or medium guns and CIWS.

THE OLIVER HAZARD PERRY
TYPE

The Oliver Hazard Perry, built between 1977 and 1988 by the US Navy, was considered as the best frigate in the world and was built under license by other countries.

During the 1950s, the US Navy built new escort ships and financed the construction of others in NATO countries such as France, Italy and Portugal.

New models
The first new model was the Dealey, followed by the Bronstein and the García, which had problems with the high-pressure steam propulsion system used. The Cloud Jones model used diesel engines. At the same time as the García, the US built the Brooke class, which, equipped with SAM Tartar, were the first escorts to carry missiles.

The Knox class
The Knox class was tremendously successful, and thirty years later some are still used by countries such as Greece and Turkey. Originally designated as OF, they were modified to FF in 1975. Spain built a variant, the Baleares class, armed with Standard SM1 MR missiles.

Peacetime damage
The appearance of the air-launched ASM missile during the Falklands War and the Iran-Iraq War, and the attack on the frigate Stark in 1987 with Exocet missiles fired from an Iraqi Mirage

F-1, showed the shortcomings of these ships, which although economic to build were robustly constructed, as shown in 1988 when the Samuel B. Roberts collided with a mine, but managed to reach port although damaged.

The Oliver H. Perry

The FFG are propelled by LM 2.500 gas turbines, with one shaft and five variable pitch propellers, plus 350 CV auxiliary electric retractable propellers to help with docking maneuvers. They were the first US Navy anti-submarine ships not to be equipped with ASROC missile torpedoes, although they launch SSM Harpoon and SAM Standard missiles.

Armament

The anti-submarine weapons are three-battery 324 mm torpedo launchers with Honeywell Mk 46 and/or Alliant / Westinghouse Mk 50 torpedoes, which can be launched by the SH-60 B LAMPS III helicopters in real-time data link with the ship.

Higher cost

The growing sophistication of the ships has modified the original conception leading to the total cost, including weapons, sensors and helicopters, being higher than first planned. The proposed number of ships was reduced due to the doubts held by the Joint Chiefs about the role of the NRF (Naval Reserve Force), which, finally received some Knox and Perry class ships to replace their Gearing training ships. The USA has begun to cede some ships to Bahrain, Egypt, Poland and Turkey.

The Adelaide

During the 1970s, the Royal Australian Navy began to replace its Leander and Rothesay class frigates, with O.H. Perry ships, which it considered the best anti-submarine frigate.

The Santa María

Spain built six FFG to act as escorts for the Príncipe de Asturias aircraft carrier.

Three similar groups

The Santa María, F-81, Victoria, F-82 and Numancia, F-83 comprised the first group. The Reina Sofía, F-84 was constructed independently. The Navarra, F-85 and Canarias, F-86 were built last and their electronic combat gear was better integrated and with more components made in Spain.

Differences with the original design

The Spanish FFG were different in some respects from the original design. The beam was increased from 13.7 to 14.3 m, with increased stability. Computer-guided stabilizer fins, CIWS Meroka systems, Selenia RAN 30L/X radar for CIWS, ESM/ECM Nettunel or Mk 3000 Neptune, spoilers (only the F-85 and F-86) in the stern which increases the range, consumption and speed and a Prairie acoustic masking system were added.

The Cheng Kung

Taiwan built some ships of this type, whose differences with the Perry lie in the weapons and systems they carry. The ships are equipped with SSM Hsiung Feng II missiles in two banks of four, and two 40/70 mm guns in consoles on either side of the hangar at the height of the OTO-Melara 76/62 mm gun. Some are also equipped with guns on the roof of the hangar and the roof of the bridge is reinforced to support the Hsiung Feng II.

RUSSIAN
FRIGATES

Since WW2, Russia has built frigates under the denomination of Neustrashymy class.

Cold War

During the Cold War, the USSR began to build a powerful navy, including the Sverdlov class cruisers, the Whiskey class submarines, the Skory class destroyers and the Riga class frigates. The first signs of this increased power in the 1950s alarmed the West, leading to a reciprocal increase in weapons building.

▼ In the Neustrashimy I frigates, the weaponry is concentrated in the bow forecastle and includes a 100/59 mm gun, four VLS with eight SAM SA-N-9 Gauntlet missiles and the ASW RBU 12,000 mortar which fires warheads of 80 kg at distances of up to 12,000 m.

▼ The ratio between the flotation length and the maximum beam, show the good navigability of the ships. The steeply raked stem with its straight line at 45⁰ to the flotation line suggests a large sonar dome in the stern.

From the Riga to the Kresta

The Riga were frigates of limited capacity (1,500 tons fully loaded) and limited freeboard, but were useful in the North Atlantic and similar inhospitable waters.

Outdated technology

The Riga used technology dating from 1940 and were armed only with 100 mm guns, some anti-air guns, torpedo launchers, mortars and A/S depth charges and mine-laying capabilities.

The Krivak are frigates performing anti-submarine duties. A number of modernized Krivak III were built for India. The picture shows a Krivak II.

The lines of the hull are clear in this photo of the Neukrotimy. The raking stem indicates that the sonar dome is in stem and the rib along part of the hull maintains the ratio between the length and beam.

New ships

The Kola project was replaced by the Riga class which was easier to build in large numbers. Both were powered by traditional steam boilers and turbines. The following class was the Petya, which entered service around 1963. Its dimensions and capacity were similar to the Riga, but with improved weaponry and electronic sensors, and was powered by two diesel engines on one shaft and two gas turbines on two shafts.

New concepts

The following classes, the Mirka, Grisha and Koni, entered service at the end of the 1970s and early 1980s. Some employed SAM SA-N-4 missiles, and they had CODAG/CODOG combined propulsion. Starting with these ships, a distinction was made between frigates and corvettes or heavy patrol ships, with or without missiles. Even so, some still considered the Kresta class, built between 1965 and 1977, as cruisers, with their official USSR denomination being heavy anti-submarine ships.

The Krivak

The following class of frigates was the Krivak, built between 1970 and 1990, with some remaining in service today. The ships had a displacement of between 3,575 and 3,900 tons, with diverse artillery, SAM SA-N-4, SSM SS-N-25 and ASW SS-N-14 missiles and RBU 6000

mortars, eight torpedo launchers for a variety of torpedoes, and mine-laying capacities. All were propelled by a COGAG system.

The Neustrashimy
The Neustrashimy is the latest class of frigate constructed in Russia. One has been in service since 1993, another may have been sold and a third is being scrapped at Kaliningrad ship-yards.

Plataform
The hull maintains many characteristic Russian elements but incorporates features from Western ships. The bow forecastle has a sheer aft in its upper third to facilitate firing of the bow gun. The deck extends for almost all the length of the ship. The helicopter hanger forms part of the stern superstructure and the VDS is housed on the raised deck.

Stealth capabilities
This is the first Russian ship to incorporate stealth capabilities, such as dihedral bulkheads, in order to avoid enemy radar.

Weaponry

The armament includes SAM SA-N-9 Gauntlet missiles with two CIWS CADS-N-1 batteries (two multi-battery guns and two four-battery SA-N-11 missiles). The torpedo launchers can fire SS-CX-5 Sapless. ASW systems include SS-N-15 and/or 16 missiles, a RBU 12,000 mortar and a multi-purpose gun.

Sensors

The array of sensors includes Top Plate and Palm Frond search and surveillance radar, Cross Sword (for the SA-N-9), Kite Screech and Hot Flash (for the CADS-N-1) fire-control radar, IFF Salt Pot and Box Bar; Bell Crown datalink arms control systems, ESM/ECM, Foot Ball, Half Hat electronic warfare systems and Half Cup laser interceptors and PK 10 and PF16 decoy launchers.

The Grisha class, of which the Grisha II is shown, were built during the 1980s and some remain in service in former Eastern Bloc countries.

THE MEKO
FRIGATES

The modular ship is designed according to needs of the client, and, while needing considerable technical effort, reduces costs.

The Turkish ship Barbaros, showing the weaponry, and especially the Harpoon batteries amidships, which are double and not qaudruple, as is the norm.

The Liberty ships and the XXI submarines

During WWI some attempts at mass naval construction were made, such as the Eagle patrol boats. However, it was not until WW2 when the Liberty merchant ship were built rapidly, by mass production methods comparable to those of the car industry. The Liberty boats were launched almost completely finished, with the engines installed. Their sturdy finish, ability to survive attacks and longevity have validated their construction system. Germany used similar methods to construct their XXI and XXIII class submarines.

Integrated construction

The development of naval construction from the 1970s onwards was centered on the mass production techniques applied in Korean and Japanese dockyards, which combined economy with quality.

Modular construction

A distinction must be made between modular construction methods and integrated modular construction. The modular design provides a common platform, whose weaponry and equipment can be tailored to the client's needs.

The modules, built and installed are transported to the finishing bays, where they are sandblasted and painted, with the final assembly taking place on the slipway.

Integrated modular construction

In the integrated modular construction process, the modules are built almost completely in the factory, arriving at the slipway sandblasted, painted, and with part of the interior elements incorporated (lighting, engines, services, living quarters, etc.) shortening construction times and cutting costs.

One characteristic of the system is that the modules are built upside-down, avoiding scaffolding and saving labor. Examples of this process are the Thai aircraft-carrier, the Chakri Naruebet built by E.N.Bazán/Izar and the Álvaro of Bazán frigates.

The MEKO

MEKO stands for MEhrzweck KOmbitation (better combination of objectives), adopted by the Hamburg dockyards Blohm & Voss and by Howaldswerke in Kiel. The first MEKO was the Nigerian frigate Aradu, which entered service in 1982.

▼ *The modules are assembled by welding and fixing of services using piping, electrical components, etc.*

Sold to many navies

Currently, MEKO ships are employed by the navies of Argentina (four MEKO 360 and five MEKO 140), Australia (six MEKO 200 ANZ), Greece (four MEKO 200 HN), Nigeria (a MEKO 360), New Zealand (two MEKO 200 ANZ), Portugal (three MEKO 200) and Turkey (four MEKO 200 and four modified MEKO 200). From 2002, six MEKO 100 OPV projected to be built in Malaysia will be delivered.

The MEKO 200

The most numerous of the MEKO ships are the MEKO 200, with four versions, the 200, 200HN, 200 ANZ and 200 modified, all with differing characteristics and performance.

The most recent models are the ANZ (Australia-New Zealand), which are on the point of delivery and should enter service between 2003 and 2006, and the oldest the Turkish 200, which entered service in 1987.

The platform

The ships have a hull with a large freeboard over which is built the superstructure from the command bridge to the hanger, including the two masts and a bifurcated funnel. The propulsion is usually CODAD or CODOG, or even COGOG.

Weaponry

Generally, the ships are armed with only one American 127 mm gun (the Portugese MEKO have French 100 mm guns and the Argentine ships an OTO-Melara 127 mm) and SSM Harpoon and/or SAM Sea Sparrow missiles in vectored or VLS eight-battery launchers.

For point defense, the Greek, New Zealand and Portugese ships use a multiple CIWS Vulcan Phalanx gun, the Turks three Oerlikon Contraves Sea Zenith guns and the Australian ships nothing. The ASW armament in all the ships is two three-barrel 324 launchers supplied with Mk 46 torpedoes.

 *The Australian Anzac are similar to the other MEKO in performance, equipment, weaponry and sensors. The differences are those imposed by the client, often motivated by political or economic reasons or technological dependence.*

Modular construction means that the modules are delivered to the slipway almost complete. All that is needed is to join them together and connect the services.

◄ The Turkish MEKO usually carry a complete load of Harpoon missiles stored amidships, unlike the Greek, Portugese, Australian and New Zealand ships. These MEKO 200 have a powerful presence, especially due to their Swiss-Italian CIWS Contraves Sea Zenith guns.

Characteristics compared (MEKO 200)						
Class/Number	Anzac (8)	Hydra (4)	Te Kaha (2)	Vasco da Gama (3)	Yavuz (4)	Barbaros (4)
Delivery	1996/2004	1992/1999	1997/1999	1991	1987/1989	1995/2000
Length/Beam/Draught	118x14.8x4.35	117x14.8x4.1	118x14.8x4.4	116x14.8x6.1	115x14.2x4.1	117x14.8x4.3
Displacement	3,600	3,200	3,600	3,300	2,920	3,350
Propulsion	CODOG	CODOG	CODOG	CODOG	CODAD	CODOG
Engines	LM 2500 (1) MTU 12V 1163 TB 83 (2)	LM 2500 (2) MTU 20V 956 TB 82 (2)	LM 2500 (1) MTU 12V 1163 TB 83 (2)	LM 2500 (2) MTU 12V 1163 TB 83 (2)	MTU 20V 1163 TB 93 (4)	LM 2500 (2) MTU 16V 1163 TB 83 (2)
Power	30,172-8,840	60,000-10,420	30,172-8,840	53,000-8.840	29,940	60,000-11,780
Speed/Range	27-6,000/18	31-20-4,100/16	27-6,000/18	32-4,900/18 20-9,600/12	27-4,100/18	32-4,100/18
Weaponry :	8 SAM/VLS Sea Sparrow RIM-7NP 1 127/54 mm Gun 2 (2x1) 12.7 mm Machine guns 6 TL ASW 324 mm (2xIII) 1 Helicopter	8 SSM Harpoon 16 SAM Sea Sparrow 1 127/54 mm Gun 2 CIWS Vulcan Phalanx 6 TL ASW 324 mm (2xIII) 1 Helicopter	8 SAM/VLS Sea Sparrow RIM-7NP 1 127/54 mm Gun 2 (2x1) 12.7 mm Machine guns 6 TL ASW 324 mm (2xIII) 1 Helicopter	8 SSM Harpoon 16 SAM Sea Sparrow 1 100/55 mm Gun 1 CIWS Vulcan Phalanx 2 Oerlikon 20 mm (2xI) Guns 6 TL ASW 324mm (2xIII) 2 Helicopters	8 SSM Harpoon 24 SAM Aspide 1 127/54 mm Gun 3 CIWS Sea Zenith 6 TL ASW 324 mm (2xIII) 1 Helicopter	8 SSM Harpoon 24 SAM Aspide 1 127/54 mm Gun 3 CIWS Sea Zenith 6 TL ASW 324 mm (2xIII) 1 Helicopter

In forthcoming years, more frigates will be built than other types of ship.

From the Atlantic to the Mediterranean

Two classes of frigates are currently in service, the Atlantic type, with corresponding performance and characteristics and the Mediterranean type, mainly Italian.

The Halifax

These frigates were originally designed as anti-submarine ships, although they possess certain multi-role characteristics.

▼ Here a logistics ship can be seen, between two modern frigates. The latter require the support of the former to extend their range and power by supplying them with fuel, weapons and stores.

▼ One of the tasks assigned to surface warships is the protection of more important and valuable ships, such as aircraft carriers. They can provide them with anti-submarine, anti-aircraft and surface protection.

Origins

In 1977, the Canadian government announced its intention to construct a group of ships known, in principle, as the Canadian Patrol Frigate. Construction contracts were signed in 1983 and 1987.

Modernization

The ships are undergoing a TIAPS (Towed Integrated Active/ Passive Sonar) upgrade and four will be converted into air-defense ships from 2002, being equipped with APAR radar and SAM Standard or ERSS (Extended Range Sea Sparrow) missiles.

General impressions

The frigates have a hull with a large freeboard and hardly any sheering, which at the extreme of the forecastle is converted into negative sheering to facilitate firing of the Bofors 57/70 mm Mk 2 gun, lighter in caliber than the normal 76/62 or 127/54 mm guns.

The superestructures consist of a very low prow structure which houses the flight deck and most of the electronic sensors, a central structure containing only the funnel and the two VLS, and another stern structure containing the CH-124 Sea King helicopter hanger with the CIWS Phalanx gun, the SATCOM antenna and the second Signaal SPG-503 (STIR 1.8) illuminator on its roof.

The VLS are located on either side of the funnel, equipped with two groups of eight large IR filters.

The Duke/Type 23

The British Duke class, Type 23 frigates were conceived as the replacements for the Leander class and the extremely expensive Type 22, but the Falklands War meant their entry into service was delayed when costs soared.

Power

The ships are powered by a CODLAG (COmbined Diesel, Electric And Gas) system combining

groups of diesel-electric and gas turbines with electric motors, which through the reduction gear, activate two variable pitch propellers.

Weaponry

The armament is mixed, one of the lessons of the Falklands War, and includes SSM Harpoon (2xIV) missiles, a 32-battery VLS SAM missile launcher with Seawolf missiles, a Vickers 114/55 m Mk-8 gun, two (2xI) Oerlikon/DES 30/75 mm Mk-1 guns, four (2xII) ASW 324 mm torpedo launchers and an ASW Sea King or EH-101 Merlin HAS 1 helicopter.

Plataform

The appearance is similar to the Halifax, with three superstructures on a topside hull. The armaments are concentrated to the bow, the bridge superstructure houses most of the sensors, with the single large funnel housing IR filters and the stern superstructure housing the helicopter hanger which supports one of the Marconi Type 911 illuminators and some arcs which are presumably part of the stealth anti-radar system.

The Italian frigates

The Italian navy currently has thirteen frigates of three distinct types; the Artigliere (4), Maestrale (8) and Lupo (1).

Artigliere and Lupo

The Artigliere, which are ships embargoed in 1992 when destined for Iraq, are Lupo class ships with some differences. The Perseo was delivered in 1980.

The ships are well-equipped for ASuW warfare, thanks to their Teseo missiles and the SAM (1 eight battery launcher with with 8+8 Aspide missiles, also operable with RIM-7M) and conventional artillery (1 OTO-Melara 127/54 mm gun and 4 Bofors/ Breda 40/ 70 mm guns) and ASW weaponry (6 324 torpedo launchers with Mk-46 torpedoes). The electronics and EW systems are of the same standard. The ships are propelled by a CODOG system with a top speed of 35 knots with turbines and 21 knots with diesel.

The Maestrale

The Maestrale, delivered between 1982 and 1985, use similar gas turbines as the Lupo but the displacement is 25% greater, the maximum speed is only 32 knots, although the cruising speed is the same at 21 knots. The range is greater, 6,000 miles at 16 knots compared to 4,350 miles at 16 knots for the Lupo.

▼ *The Maestrale are ships with ASuW and ASW capabilities, reflecting naval thinking of the time. They are still equipped with VDS instead of acoustic rastras, and with A/S 533 mm and 324 torpedoes. The photo shows the Scirocco with the hull cropped to contain the VDS.*

▶ *Designs that appeared in the final decades of the last century have extensive superstructures mounting all types of systems, equipment and weapons, while designs that are more recent tend towards cleaner, stealthier shapes.*

Plataforms compared

The three types have a similar look, with a main deck running from the stern to the transom, with pronounced sheering, a central superstructure from side to side at bridge height, an aft superstructure under the flight deck and another superstructure housing the command bridge, the weapons, sensors, funnel and helicopter hangar.

Armament

The weaponry of the Maestrale is composed of four SSM Teseo Mk 2 (TG2) missiles, 16 Aspide SAM (8+8) missiles in a battery of eight, an OTO-Melaraf 127/54 mm gun, four Bofors/Breda 40/70 mm guns, two Oerlikon 20 or 25 mm guns, six 324 mm torpedo launchers with Mk 46 torpedoes, two 533 torpedo launchers (in the stem)

with Whitehead A184 torpedoes. The Lupo has 16 SSM Teseo missiles but no 533 mm torpedo launchers.

Electrical equipment

The electronic sensors of the Maestrale include Selenia SPS-774 (RAN 10S) air and surface-search radar operating in bands E/F; SMA SPS-702 surface-search radar in band I; SMA SPN-703 navegation radar in band I; Selenia SPG-75 (RTN 30X) fire-control radar for the SAM and 127 mm gun in bands I/J and two Selenia SPG-74 (RTN 20X) for the 40/70 guns in bands I/J; IFF Mk XII; NA-30 arms-control systems for the SAM and 127 mm gun; two Dardo for the 40/70 mm guns; IPN 20 (SADOC 2) combat system; datalink 11; SATCOM, and two AB 212 ASW helicopters.

Characteristics compared

Performance:	Halifax	Duke/123	Maestrale	Brandenburg	Karel Doorman
Class/number	Halifax (12)	Duke/123 (16)	Maestrale (8)	Brandenburg (4)	Karel Doorman (8)
Delivery	1991/1996	1990/2002	1982/1985	1994/1996	1991/1995
Length/beam/draught	135x16.4x7.1	133x16.1x7.3	123x12.9x4.6	139x16.7x6.8	122x14.4x4.3
Displacement	4,770	4,200	3,200	4,700	3,320
Propulsion	CODOG	CODLAG	CODOG	CODOG	CODOG
Engines	LM 2500 (2) SEMT-Pielstick20 PA6 V280 (1)	Spey SM1A/C (2) Paxman 12CM(4) GEC (2)	LM 2500 (2) GMT BL 230.20 DVM (2)	LM 2500SA (2) MTU 20V 956 TB 92 (2)	Spey SM1C (2) Stork-Wärtsila 12SW280 (2)
Power	47,494/8,800 CV	31,100/8,100 CV	50,000/12,600 CV	51,000/11,070 CV	33,800/9,790 CV
Speed/range	29	28	32/21	29/18	30/21
	3,930/18-9,500/15	4,000/15-7,800/15	6,000/16	4,000/18	5,000/18
Weaponry:	8 SSM Harpoon (2xIV)	8 SSM Harpoon (2xIV)	4 SSM Teseo Mk2 (TG2) (4xI)	4 SSM Exocet MM 38 (2xII)	8 SSM Harpoon
	16 SAM Sea Sparrow VLS (2xVIII)	32 SAM/PDMS Seawolf VLS	16 SAM Aspide	16 SAM Sea Sparrow VLS	16 SAM Sea Sparrow VLS
	1 57/70 mm Gun	1 114/55 mm Gun	1 127/54 mm Gun	2 RAM PDMS (2xI)	1 OTO Melara 76/62 mm Gun
	1 CIWS Vulcan Phalanx	2 30/75 mm (2xI) Guns	4 40/70 mm (2xII) Guns	1 OTO Melara 76/62 mm Gun	1 CIWS Goalkeeper
	8 12.7 mm Machine Guns	4 TL ASW 324 mm (2xII)	2 Oerlikon 20 mm (2xI)	2 Rheimetall 20 mm (2xI)	2 Oerlikon 20 mm (2xI)
	4 TL ASW 324 mm (2xII)	1 Helicopter	6 TL ASW 324 mm (2xIII)	4 TL ASW 324 mm (2xII)	4 TL ASW 324 mm (2xII)
	1 Helicopter		2 TL ASW 533 mm (2xI)	2 Helicopters	1 Helicopter
			1 Helicopter		

CURRENT AND FUTURE
FRENCH FRIGATES

The French Navy currently disposes of the most modern frigates, the Floréal and La Fayette, which, in some years will be joined by the Horizon, a joint project with Italy.

A notable achievement

Since the advent of stealth technology, many countries have tried to incorporate these capabilities in their ships. The first country to achieve real results was France, with the technologically advanced La Fayette class (La Fayette, Surcouf, Courbet, Aconit and Guépratte).

Export success

In 1991, France authorized the sale of 16 ships to Taiwan. Six were built, while the remaining ten will be changed for 1,500 ton corvettes which are cheaper to build. Saudi Arabia has ordered three ships, the Al Riyadh, Makkah and Al Dammam, which are somewhat different to the original design. The first has been delivered and the remaining two are scheduled for 2003 and 2004.

The La Fayette frigates
The absence of exterior elements give them an unfinished feel. Everything that could produce a radar echo has been protected behind bulkheads or screens, even the boat decks located laterally amidships.

Double hull
The La Fayette are built of stressed steel, and have a double hull from the water line to the deck as added protection against missiles. The hulls are separated by passages or service galleries, some duplicated to ensure operational effectiveness if part of the ship is damaged by missiles.

Special characteristics
The essential elements are protected by steel armor plate and the main deck has a long, wide corridor (jokingly called "Les Champs Elysées") which gives direct access to the holds. The funnels and higher parts of the ship are constructed of a mixture of balsa wood and GRP, treated with fire-resistant materials. The side panels of the 100/55 mm Mod 68 CADAM system are built the same way.

Armament
The ships possess relatively poor conventional weapons, with only a 100/55 mm gun, another Giat 20F2 20 mm in each bridge aileron and two 12.7 mm machine guns.
The missiles include two four-battery SSM Exocet MM40, an eight-barrel SAM Crotale Naval and are scheduled to be fitted with a VLS de16 Aster 15, in a modification which will include Arabel radar and SAAM (Système naval d'autodéfense moyen portée). At present they have

The ailerons of the bridge house Giat 20F2 20 mm light guns with a firing-rate of 720 shots/minute and a range of 10 km. The hinged gunwale follows the inclination of the superstructure bulkhead. Everything is protected behind bulkheads, such as the transponder of the gyroscope, the 20 mm 20F2 guns, the life rafts and the CSEE Dagaie Mk 2 decoy launchers.

The stealth capabilities of the LaFayette frigates have been optimized. The forecastle has been covered with entry gained by flaps which are closed during sailing and open when docking maneuvers begin. The tower of the DCN 100/55 mm Mod 68 CADAM gun has been designed with balsa wood additions for camouflage.

◄ A metal mesh protects the life-boats and their launching gear which are difficult to hide.

▼ All the mooring systems on the aft superstructure are located under the deck behind protective bulkheads, with access provided by special tailgates.

LA FAYETTE

The Crotale Naval point defense system is formed by eight missiles and sensors. The missiles are loaded automatically from the cargo hatch on the deck. The Thomson CFS Sea Tiger Mk 2 air and surface-search radar is housed on the top of the stern funnel. At the stern, the gas exhausts are protected by diffusing panels and IR filters.

no anti-submarine weapons except for the AS 565 MA Panther helicopter, which may be replaced by a Super Frelon. The flight deck is equipped with a SAMAHE system with an automatic trolley and a Beartrap anchoring system.

Sensors

The electronics include Thomson-CSF Sea Tiger Mk2 air and surface-search radar in bands E/F, which detects targets as small as 2 m²; two Racal-Decca 1.229, with one controlling the helicopter in band I; Thomson-CSF Castor 2J, band J fire-control radar detecting targets of only 1 m²; Thomson-CSF CTM radar/IR arms control; Sagem TDS 90 VIGY optronics; Thomson-CSF TAVITAC 2,000 combat data systems; two SATCOM Syracuse; and OPSMER command support. Countermeasures include two CSEE Dagaie Mk2 decoy launchers and ESM Thomson-CSF ARBR-17systems.

The Floréal

The Floréal are considered as ocean patrol ships or surveillance frigates. They have seen service guarding the French colonies such as the French West Indies, Numea, the Indian Ocean and Tahiti since 1992. Their weaponry includes SSM Exocet missiles, a 100/55 mm gun and two 20 mm Oerlikon. The Dagaie decoy launchers will probably be replaced by SAM Matra Simbad missiles.

The future plans of the navies of many Asian countries are centered on escort ships like the frigate.

China

The current Chinese fleet has modern, well-equipped ships. Although their true performance is still secret, they should not be underestimated. In addition to their fleet of strategic and attack missile nuclear submarines and those in the reserve, the Chinese are constructing others with the aid of Russian technicians. Added to these are the three conventional Chinese-built submarines (with two more scheduled for delivery in 2004) as well as four Kilo class ships.

The Luhu Frigates

The Haribing and Qingdao frigates comprise the Luhu class. The ships have CODOG pro-pulsion, with the Haribing using LM 2.500 and the Qingdao Ukraine gas turbines, giving a maximum speed of 31 knots, with German MTU diesel engines.

Armament and sensors

The SSM armaments include Chinese-made YJ-1 (Eagle Strike) CSS-N-4 Sardine or CSS-8-Saccade subsonic sea-skimming missiles, SAM CSA-4 in with a HQ-7 container (a Chinese copy of the Crotale). In addition they have a double bank of 100/56 mm guns and four double banks of 37/63 guns. The ASW armaments include two triple Whitehead B515 324 mm torpedo launchers with Mk 46 mod 1 torpedoes, 12-battery rocket-laun-

◀ Pakistan's Navy has acquired modern warships from countries like the UK. Here are two of their 'Tariq' class frigates, exercising jointly with an American warship, in the background. These formerly Type 21 'Amazon' class ships were received within the last decade.

▶ The Indian Godavari of which four are in service are of British design with differences in the funnel, stern, hawse and aft superstructure and use Russian arms such as the SSM launchers on the forecastle. Two ships will be equipped with four-battery SSM SS-N-25 missiles instead of single SS-N-2D.

ching mortars, and two Harbin Zhi-9 A Haitun helicopters (a Chinese copy of the French Dauphin 2).

The sensors, electronic countermeasures and electronic warfare systems contain both Chinese and Western elements.

The Jiangwei Frigates

The Jiangwei Frigates (Anoing, Huainan, Huaibei and Tongling) were delivered between 1991 and 1994. Like the Luhu class an export version was also constructed.

Performance

The displacement of 2,250 tons fully loaded is less than the Luhu. The ships are armed with six SSM YJ-1 (Eagle Strike) missiles and SAM RF-61 (CSA-N-2). The artillery is the same as the Luhu. For ASW they only have two RBU 1200 rocket launchers and a Harbin

Zhi-9 A helicopter. Part of the electronics and the decoy launchers are Western.

The Luda Frigates

The Luda class was the first Chinese design, although it was based on the Russian Kotlin destroyers. The complete series includes 15 ships, which entered service between 1971 and 1991. There are two versions, one with a helicopter flight deck and hangar and another with artillery in the stern.

The ships have a displacement of 3,600 tons fully loaded, and are equipped with SSM HY-2/CSS- C-3 A Seersucker and SAM CSA-4 missiles in HQ-7 containers.

India

India has one of the largest fleets in Asia, mainly consisting of ceded British or Russian ships, although in the last fifteen years it has

been building its own ships based on British or Russian designs. India is a strategically important country, both because of the tensions existing with Pakistan and because it possesses nuclear weapons.

The Nilgiri Frigates

The Nilgiri are Indian-built but are an almost-direct copy of the British Leander class, and are now outdated in spite of periodic upgrading. They are propelled by conventional steam boilers and turbines.

They possess conventional artillery and anti-submarine weapons and a helicopter housed in a retractable hanger.

The Godavari Frigates

In the 1970s, India built half a dozen Leander class frigates under license. The ships were delivered between 1974 and 1981, and were

The Thai Chao Phraya, officially corvettes although with frigate markings, are similar to the Chinese Jiang-hu IV and V frigates. On arrival in Thailand they were forced to undergo substantial repairs.

a copy (Nilgiri class) with adapted armament and sensors.

Indian-designed ships

In the late 1970s, India designed the Project 16 or Godavari class, based on the Leander class. These had adapted armament and sensors, but the hull and propulsion remained the same, with steam boilers and turbines. Two ships, the Brahmaputra and Betwa have been delivered and the third is scheduled for 2004.

Another, more modern, Indian-built design is the Talwar whose series will be completed by deliveries in 2003 and 2006.

Thailand

Thailand has naval interests in the Andaman Sea, the Gulf of Kompong and the South China Sea, separated by the Straits of Malacca. The Thai navy is expanding and has been reinforced by the Chakri Naruebet aircraft carrier and Naresuan and Chao Phraya frigates during the last decade.

The Naresuan Frigates

The Chinese-built Naresuan and Taksin were delivered in 1994 and 1995 and can be considered as smaller, modified versions of the Luhu class.

Electronics

The array of electronic sensors, countermeasures and EW equipment is of mixed origin. The Signaal LW 08 air-search radar is Dutch, the Type 360 ground-search radar is Chinese, the Raytheon SPS-64(V)5 navigation radar is American, the fire-control

▼ *The Thai Naresuan are Chinese built and designed, but the 127 mm and SSM artillery are American and the electronics American and Dutch.*

radar for the SSM and 127 mm gun is a Signaal STIR and for the 37 mm guns is a Chinese type 374G, as is the SJD-7 sonar. The countermeasures are 26-battery Chinese 945 GPJ and the ESM/ECM Elettronica Newton Beta EW system is Italian.

Frigates

The Chinese-built Chao Phraya were delivered in 1991 and 1992 and are smaller then the Naresuan with diesel propulsion. There are two versions, one with 100/56 mm artillery in the bow and stern and the other with a helicopter hanger. The artillery, part of the electronics and the SSM and SAM missiles are Chinese.

Other frigates

Various other countries also possess frigates such as South Korea with the Ulsan class and Indonesia with the Fatahillah.

▼ The Pakistani Zulfiquar was originally the British Apollo, Leander class frigate. Many older ships are still in service thanks to their purchase by smaller navies.

▶ Geographically, most of Turkey lies in Asia. Its navy contains ships of various origins, such as the American Oliver H. Perry frigates. Pictured is the Gemlik, ex-Flatley.

Performance:	Luhu	Jiangwei I	Jiangwei II	Nilgiri	Godavari
Class/Number	Luhu (2)	Jiagwei I (4)	Jiangwei II (3)	Nilgiri (5)	Godavari (6)
Delivery	1994/1996	1991/1994	1998/1999	1974/1981	1983/2003
Length/Beam/Draught	143x15.1x5.1	112x12.1x4.8	112x12.1x4.8	113x13x5.5	127x14.5x4.5
Displacement	4,200	2,250	2,250	2,682	3,850
Propulsion	CODOG	Diesel	Diesel	Steam 850°/38 Kg/cm²	Steam 850°/38 Kg/cm²
Engines	LM 2500 (2) o Ukraine (2) MTU 12V 1163 TB 83 (2)	12E 390 (2)	12E 390 (2)	Turbines (2)	Turbines (2)
Power	48,600/8,840	14,400 CV	14,400 CV	30,000 CV	30,000 CV
Speed/range	31-5,000/15	25-4,000/18	25-4,000/18	27-4,500/12	27-4,500/12
Weaponry:	8 SSM YJ-1 Eagle Strike 8 SAM HQ-7 (Crotale) 2 100/56 mm (2xII) Guns 8 37/63 Type 76 A (4xII) Guns 6 TL ASW 324 mm (3xII) 2 ASW FQF 2500 (2xXII) Mortars 2 Harbin Zhi-9A Haifun Helicopters	6 SSM YJ-1 Eagle Strike 6 SAM RF-91 (CSA-N-2) 2 100/56 mm (1xII) Guns 8 37/63 Type 76A (4xII) Guns 2 ASW RUB 1200 (2xV) mortars 1 Harbin Zhi-9A Haifun Helicopter	6 SSM YJ-1 Eagle Strike 6 SAM RF-91 (CSA-N-2) 2 100/56 mm (1xII) Guns 8 37/63 Type 76A (4xII) Guns 2 ASW RUB 1200 (2xV) mortars 1 Harbin Zhi-9a Haifun Helicopters	2 114/45 mm (1xII) Guns 4 30/65 mm (2xII) AK 230 Guns 2 Oerlikon 20/70 (2xI) 6 TL ASW 324 mm (2xIII) 1 ASW Bofors 375 (1xII) Mortar 1 Helicopter	4 SSM SS-N-2D Styx 20 SAM SA-N-4 Gecko 2 57/70 mm (1xII) Guns 8 30/65 mm (4xII) AK 230 Guns 6 TL ASW 324 mm (2xIII) 2 Helicopters

Performance:	Talwar	Naresuan	Chao Phraya	Ulsan	Fatahillah
Class/Number	Talwar (4)	Naresuan (2)	Chao Phraya (4)	Ulsan (9)	Fatahillah (3)
Delivery	2002/2006	1994/1995	1991/1992	1981/1993	1979/1980
Length/Beam/Draught	124.5x15.2x4.2	120x13x3.8	103x11.3x3.1	102x11.5x3.5	84x11.1x3.3
Displacement	3,250	2,980	1,924	2,180	1,450
Propulsion	COGAG	CODOG	Diesel	CODOG	CODOG
Engines	M8 KF (2) M62 (2)	LM 2500 (2) MTU 20V 1163 TB83 (2)	MTU 20V 1163 TB83 (4)	LM 2500 (2) MTU 16V 538) TB82 (2)	Olympus TM3B MTU 20V 956 TB92 (2)
Power	43,283/12,000 CV	44,250/11,780 CV	29,440 CV	53,640/5,940 CV	25,440/11,070 CV
Speed/range	32-4,500/18	32-4,000/18	30-3,500/18	34-4,000/15	30-4,250/16
Weaponry:	8 SSM SS-N-27 Novator 24 SAM SA-N-7 Gadfly 2 CADS-N-1 1 100/59 mm Gun 4 PTA-53 533 mm Torpedoes 1 RBU 6,000 mortar	8 SSM Harpoon 8 SAM Sea Sparrow VLS 1 127/54 mm Gun 4 37/76 mm Guns 6 TL ASW 324 mm (2xIII) 1 Helicopter	8 SSM YJ-1 Eagle Strike 2 or 4 100/56 mm Guns 8 37/63 Type 76A (4xII) Guns 2 ASW RUB 1200 (2xV) Mortars 1 Helicopter (in the 2/100)	8 SSM Harpoon 2 OTO Melara 76/62 mm (2xI) 6 Breda 40/70 mm (3xII) 6 TL ASW of 324 mm (2xIII) 12 A/S Depth charges	4 SSM MM38 Exocet 1 Bofors 120/46 mm Gun 2 40/70 mm (2xI) Guns 2 Rheinmetall 20 mm (2xI) 6 TL ASW 324 mm (2xIII) 1 ASW Bofors 375 (1xII) Mortar 1 Helicopter

Historically, corvettes have been considered as a lesser category than frigates. During WW2, corvettes were the usual escorts for merchant convoys.

The role of the corvette

Today's corvette is an escort ship smaller than a frigate and conceived more for escort than warfare, although corvettes with a displacement of up to 1,500 tons have been built, some of which are equipped with powerful anti-ship, anti-missile, anti-air or anti-submarine weapons.

The future of the corvette

Currently there are some forty classes of corvette on active service in different navies, ranging from combat ships to those designed for patrol, surveillance and control missions. Some are still in the design stage and may not actually be built.

Among the corvettes sailing today, the Russian Tarantul and Nanuchka, the Indian Khukri, the Malaysian Laksamana, the Singaporean Victory and the Swedish Visby class ships are modern designs adapted to current naval needs.

Tarantul (Russia)

These agile and powerful ships were constructed between 1978 and 1997 and were exported to Bulgaria, India, Poland, Rumania, Vietnam and Yemen as well as serving in the Russian and Ukranian fleets. The Russians have given them two denominations, malvy raketny korabl' (MRK/small missile ship) and raketny kater (missile cutter).

Performance

The Tarantul have a displacement of 455 tons fully loaded, with COGAG (Nikolaiev DR 76 and DR 77 turbines) or CODOG (two diesel CM 504 replacing the group of cruiser turbines in the Tarantul III) propulsion. Their top speed of 36 knots makes them among the fastest corvettes afloat.

◀ ▼ *The Moroccan Navy has one 'Descubierta' class corvette, which was built in Spanish shipyards. The ship is of a design more suited to the Mediterranean Sea than to the Atlantic Ocean.*

▼ *The LCS (Littoral Combat Ship) implies a very interesting renewal of technology and capabilities, which will lead to substantial changes in warship design in the decades to come.*

Armament

The weaponry varies according to the class, with the I and II equipped with four SSM SS-N-2D Styx and the Tarantul III with SS-N-22 Sunburn. The anti-air defense comprises SAM SA-N-5 Grail and a gun on the forecastle in all ships. The AK 630 system is replaced by a CADS-N-1 in the Tarantul II.

Electronics

The electronics also vary although most ships use Plank Shave air and surface-search radar, Kivach III navegation radar and Bass Tilt fire-control radar. The ships are equipped with Hood Wink, Light Bulb, Band Stand and Bell Nest arms control systems, IFF High Pole systems, ESM Foot Ball and/or Hard Hat sonar and PK 16 or PK 10 countermeasures.

The Nanuchka (Russia)

The Nanuchka were built between 1969 and 1991, before the Tarantul, and displace 660 tons fully loaded. Some were ceded to Algeria, India and Libya. Their classification was the same as the Tarantul. Currently, 24 ships (6 Nanuchka I/Burya, 17 III/Veter and 1 IV/Nakat) are employed by the Russian navy for coastal duties.

Propulsion

The Nanuchka are diesel-powered, with six M 504 engines driving three shafts and three propellers, giving a top speed of 33 knots.

Armament

The missiles include six SSM SS-N-9 Siren in two triple batteries (the Nanuchka IV has SS-N-25 missiles), with a double SAM SA-N-4 Gecko launcher (some ships have AsuW capacities with a cargo of 20 missiles). The artillery comprises two 57/80 mm guns (Nanuchka I) or one 76/60 gun (Nanuchka III and IV). The III and IV are equipped with an AK 630 CIWS.

Eilat (Israel)

The Eilat class comprises three American designed and built ships delivered in 1996 and 1997. They have advanced stealth features, with inclined planes in all the superstructures, a funnel with a gas cooler, abundant uses of RAM material, resilient engine mountings, and water jets for NBC warfare. The hull is of steel and the superstructure of aluminum.

Propulsion

The ships have a CODOG propulsion with an LM 2.500 turbine, two MTU diesel engines and two Kamewa variable pitch propellers.

Armament and electronics

The SSM armament is Harpoon missiles; the SAM armament is two VLS with Barak missiles. The ships have an OTO Melara 76/62 mm Compatto gun which can be replaced by a Bofors 57 mm or a CIWS Vulcan Phalanx, two CIWS Sea Vulcan 25 mm guns and six ASW 324 mm torpedo launchers with Honeywell Mk 46 torpedoes.

Khukri (India)

The Indian designed and built Khukri entered service in 1989. Problems with the supply of Russian parts delayed delivery of three ships. About 65% of the components are Indian, including the diesel engines built under license from France. The ships are equipped with stabilizing fins and air-conditioning.

Armament

The first ships were equipped with SSM SS-N-2D Styx, which are scheduled to be replaced by SS-N-25 in the second batch, in addition to SAM SA-N-5 Grail. The artillery comprises a Russian AK 176 gun and two CIWS AK 630 batteries.

Laksamana (Malaysia)

The Laksamana were built in Italy, having been ordered by Iraq in 1981 to form the Assad class, but were embargoed after the invasion of Kuwait. The weapons and sensors are completely different from those normally used by the Malaysian navy, causing maintenance problems.

Armament

The missiles include six SSM OTO Melara/Matra Otomat Teseo Mk 2 (TG2) and eight SAM Aspide. The artillery comprises an OTO Melara Compatto 76/62 mm gun and two Breda/ Bofors 40/70 mm guns, as well as two triple TL ASW 324 mm. The electronics are almost totally Italian except for the Kelvin Hughes 1,007 radar and the Atlas sonar.

Victory (Singapore)

The Victory are German-designed MGB 62, with the prototype being constructed in Germany and the rest in Singapore. They are similar to the Bahrain (Al Manama) and United Arab Emirates (Muray Jib) ships.

Performance

The ships have integral diesel propulsion with stabilizing fins and a maximum speed of 35 knots.

Armament

The Victory are armed with SSM Harpoon (8) and SAM Barak (16) missiles, a knots OTO Melara 76/62 mm gun, four 12.7 mm machine-guns and 6 ASW 324 mm torpedo launchers with Whitehead A-244 S torpedoes.

Rattanakosin (Tailandia)

The Rattanakosin of American design and construction displace 960 tons and have a length of 76.8 m. The propulsion is supplied by two German MTU diesel engines. They are extremely well armed in relation to their small capacity, being equipped with SSM Harpoon missiles, 24 SAM Aspide with an eight-battery launcher, an OTO Melara 76/62 mm gun, two Breda 40/70

guns, two Oerlikon 20 mm guns and A/S 324 mm torpedo launchers.

Visby (Sweden)

One Visby class ship has been delivered with four more scheduled for 2004 and 2006. The experience learned from the Smyge advanced technology ship has been applied, and stealth technology incorporated. The Visby are conceived as ASW/MCM ships and others with AsuW capabilities are planned. The displacement is 620 tons fully loaded, with a length of 72 m, a beam of 10.4 m and a draught of 2.5 m.

Propulsion

The ships use a CODOG propulsion system with gas turbines, diesel engines and Kamewa water jets. The maximum speed is 35 knots, with a cruising speed of 15 knots using the diesel engines.

Armament and sensors

The ships are equipped with 8 SSM RBS 15 Mk II, 1 Bofors 57/70 mm gun, 4 ASW 400 mm torpedo launchers, an ASW Saab Alecto 601 127 mm mortar and mine-laying capabilities.

Defense systems include chaff launchers, MCMV STN Atlas Seafox Combat systems, ESM/ECM Condor Systems CS 701, Ericsson Sea Giraffe 3D air and surface search radar, Celsius Tech Pilot surface-search radar and CEROS 200 Mk3 fire-control radar.

During the next ten to fifteen years, new ships classified as frigates but with vastly improved performance will enter service.

Laser weapons are still not considered operational in spite of the successful downing of a missile during a test in November 2002. However, ships with electric power which will reduce fuel consumption and allow laser weapons to be used are being designed and built.

The CNGF and TFC
NATO currently has two important projects underway; the CNGF (common new-generation frigate) in which France, Italy and the United Kingdom are participating and the TFC (Trilateral Frigate Cooperation) which includes Germany, Spain and Holland.
Both projects are developing the APAR (Active Phased ARray) European phased radar, in addition to MFR multifunction radar and data link systems, although the availability of the electronic and weapons systems are delaying the project.

Three different projects
In light of these problems, Spain decided that its F-100 would use a simplified version of the AEGIS/ SPY-1, without abandoning the APAR which may be used in the F-110. Germany opted for its own F-124 project, and Holland for its De Zeven Provincien.
Meanwhile, the CNGF has evolved into the Horizon project although the United Kingdom withdrew and designed its own Type 45.
At the same time, various other projects are emerging, of which the most important are the German MEKO A-200 and the Sea Wraith II, Demonstrator and Cougar, and the Triton, a futuristic trimaran which may have potential as a military ship.

◀ F-101 Alvaro de Bazán is the first of four multi-purpose frigates delivered to the Spanish Navy between 2002 and 2006. Their main strength lies in the mounting of the AEGIS system in a ship displacing less than six thousand tonnes.

▼ The angular dihedric stealth lines can be clearly seen in this photo of the Sachsen, F-219. The SAM missiles are housed in a 32-battery VLS between the bridge and the bow RAM containers (the other is located on the roof of the hanger). The Harpoon missiles are located amidships. The artillery consists of a 76/62 gun on the forecastle and two Mauser 27 mm guns.

The De Zeven Provincien

The Dutch De Zeven Provincien ships will enter service shortly. Although they were conceived as frigates, recent information classifies them as destroyers.

Plataform

The three ships whose construction is most advanced will be those with the largest displacement.

The design of the ship incorporates stealth features with emphasis on reduction of radar cross section, infrared, acoustic, electrical and magnetic signatures.

Four funnels in two groups of two and a bow of greater height than the stern gives them a singular aspect.

Armament

Their weapons include SSM Harpoon, SAM Evolved Sea Sparrow and Standard SM2-MR Block IIIA missiles with a forty-battery VLS. The artillery comprises a 127/54 mm OTO-Breda gun on the forecastle, with two CIWS Goalkeeper over the bridge and hangar, plus two Oerlikon 20 mm.

ASW systems include torpedoes launched from double fixed-launchers on either side and the Lynx helicopter.

Sensors

The array of sensors includes Signaal SMART L 3D air-search radar, the APAR fire-control radar and the Scout navigation and surface-surveillance system, IFF Mk XII, ESM/ECM Racal Sabre and SBROC Mk 36 countermeasures.

The F-100

The F-100, excellent frigates, although considered as destroyers by some. One ship, the Álvaro de Bazán is in service, with the Almirante Juan de Borbón, Blas de Lezo and Méndez Núñez, scheduled for 2003, 2004 and 2006.

Design

The project is totally Spanish, and the ships are constructed by Izar in the El Ferrol shipyards. The success of this Spanish naval technology has led Norway to choose the company to design and construct the Fridtjof Nansen class.

Plataform

The main platform is of high-tension steel or AH-36, with some areas constructed of DH-55. Parts of the deck are reinforced. The structural configuration is based on a hull with stealth properties, with a main deck which covers the length of the ship including the flight deck, under which are the second, first and sentinel decks, with the first deck also covering the whole length of the superstructure.

The F-124

The F-124 are considered as air-defense ships. Three are programmed to be built in Hamburg, Kiel and Emden.

They are an evolution of the Brandenburg frigates with data bus distribution technology, phase panel multifunction radar and ESSM, RAM and SM-2 missiles.

Platform

The exterior aspect is similar to the De Zeven Provincien, with a 76/62 mm gun and a group of bifurcated funnels, but the speed, range and CODAG propulsion with one gas turbine are different.

The Horizon

The French have commissioned two ships to enter service in 2006 and 2008, with another two probable ships being ready between 2010 and 2015. The Italians have scheduled two ships for 2007 and 2009. The program may be delayed as the weapons and electronic sensor systems are still under development.

◀ The Álvaro de Bazán class (Álvaro de Bazán, Almirante Juan de Borbón, Blas de Lezo and Méndez Núñez) have a performance and configuration different from the Dutch and German ships. The first entered service in 2002. The photo shows the Álvaro de Bazán during sea-testing.

▼ The main differences between the Spanish F-100 and the other two European frigates are in the location of the phase panels, which in the Spanish ships are situated on the superstructure and in the others on high on a polyhedral tower.

Displacement and propulsion
The Horizon ships will have a displacement of around 6,500 tons fully loaded, with a maximum length of about 150 m. The propulsion will be CODLAG or CODLOG, with two propellers, a maximum sustainable speed of 30 knots and a range of 7,000 miles at 18 knots.

Armament
The weaponry, which will vary according to the country, will include a SAM PAAMS (Principal Anti-Air Missile System) with Aster 15 and Aster 30 missiles in one VLS. This is in addition to SSM, ANNG missiles on the French ships, Teseo Mk 3 missiles on the Italian ones, and as yet unknown missiles on the British ships.
The planned artillery will consist of an AsuW gun, with two small 20 or 30 mm guns.

The Daring
The United Kingdom is constructing ships considered as destroyers with the names of Daring, Dauntless, Diamond, Dragon, Defender and Duncan, which will enter service from 2007.

▼ Similar to the Norwegian Fridtjof Nansen are the Horizon, which will serve in the French and Italian navies, and the British Type 45 destroyer. The photo shows an artist's impression of what the Common New Generation Frigate may look like.

▶ Over the next few decades, designs will be developed very much more advanced than those currently in service. Work is being done on shapes that enable warships to evade detection, on highly advanced weapons systems and on a reduction in the number of crewmembers.

Characteristics compared

Performance:	De Zeven Provincien	Álvaro de Bazán	Sachsen	Horizon	Daring
Class/Number	De Zeven P. (4)	Álvaro de B. (4)	Sachsen (3)	Horizon (4)	Daring (6)
Delivery	2002/2005	2002/2006	2003/2005	2006/2009	2007/2011
Length/Beam/Draught	144.2x18.8x5.2	146.7x18.6x4.9	143x17.4x4.4	151.6x17.5x5.1	152.4x21.2x5.3
Displacement	6,048 tones	5,853 tones	5,600 tones	6,700 tones	7,350 tones
Propulsion	CODOG	CODOG	CODAG	CODOG	IEP
Engines	SM 1C Spey (2) Störk Wartsila 16 V 26 ST (2 diesel)	GE LM 2500 (2) Bazán-Caterpillar Diesel (2)	GE LM 2500 (1) MTU 20V 1163 TB 93 diesel (2)	GE LM 2500 (2) SEMT-Pielstick Diesel (2)	RR WR 21 (2) turbo-alternators
Power	52,300/13,600 CV	47,328/12,240 CV	31,514/20,128 CV	58,480/10,880 CV	42 MW
Speed/range	28-5,000/18	28-4,500/18	29-4,000/18	29-7,000/18	29-7,000/18
Weaponry:	8 SSM Harpoon SAM Standard SM 2-MR and ESSM 1 127/54 Gun 2 CIWS Goalkeeper 2 Oerlikon 20 mm 4 TL ASW 324 mm 1 Lynx Helicopter	8 SSM Harpoon Block II SAM Standard SM 2-MR and ESSM 1 127/54 Gun 1 CIWS MEROKA 2 Oerlikon 20 mm 4 TL ASW 324 mm 1 SH-60B Seahawk LAMPS III Helicopter	8 SSM Harpoon SAM Standard SM2-MR and ESSM SAM RAM 1 76/62 Gun 2 Mauser 27 mm 6 TL ASW 324 mm 2 NFH 90 or Lynx Helicopters	8 SSM Exocet/ Teseo SAM Aster 15 and 30 3 76/62 mm Guns 2 25 mm Guns 4 TL ASW 324 mm 1 Merlin or NH-90 Helicopter	8 Harpoon SAM PAAMS Aster 15 and Aster 30 1 114/55 Gun 2 CIWS Vulcan Phalanx 2 30 mm Guns 1 Lynx or Merlin Helicopter

Photo Credits

US Navy:
7, 8, 9, 10, 11, 23, 24, 25, 26, 27, 28, 29, 34, 43, 45, 48, 49, 54, 69, 71, 73, 77, 78, 84, 85, 89, 90

Camil Busquets:
12, 14, 15, 31, 37, 38, 39, 44, 46, 47, 51, 52, 60, 62, 63, 66, 67, 72, 76, 82

Lluis Adell:
16, 18, 20, 21, 58, 75

Canada Ministry of Defense:
22, 68

H&L van Ginderen:
33, 57, 59

Chris Sattler:
35, 50, 55, 64, 66, 79

Marc Piché:
36, 82

Jorge Flethes:
80, 81

Izar:
92, 93

Remaining photographies:
HDW, Northrop Grumman, Marine Française/Marius Bar, Thales, Camil Busquets, Octavio Díez, Australian Ministry of Defense, Armada Española, Michael Winter, Antonio Moreno, Diego Quevedo, Kockhums, Izar, Marconi, General Dynamics.